Tails & Verse from Over the Hill

Creative Verse © by Miles Robertson
Design and Illustrations © by Andrew Partridge

First published 2015 by Angus Garratt Publishing
Porlock, Somerset

Printed in Great Britain by
Biddles, King's Lynn, Norfolk, PE32 1SF

ISBN: 978-0-9933871-0-4

Tails & Verse
FROM
OVER the HILL

Dedicated to
The Robertson
&
Partridge Families

Inspired by the people who live on Exmoor
...and those that visit.

Cheers.

Contents

Every picture tells a story
Preface

It is, I've found, normal at this stage,
Of most good books, and upon this page,
To write some words, a sort of intro',
Giving readers some background info'.

It helps one to accept the humour,
Or lack of it, as has been rumoured,
Of the two quite mad protagonists,
Who have strived hard to produce all this.

This book is formed from blood, sweat & tears
With much debate and a few ideas,
Plus scrunched up notes just strewn all around
The outcome is, nothing too profound.

Take the blend of two artistic minds
Like coffee beans of different kinds,
The artist and the wordsmith unite
To draw and paint and scribble and write.

The Concept

from the 'Artist Graphic',
Pictorial anthropomorphic ,*
And set to words by a logophile
In a rambling, loose and rhyming style.

The Pictures

though are things of beauty,
Drawn from the heart and not by duty,
From the drawer marked 'Life', ideas propelled,
Take their form through sharpened pencils held.

Whilst coffee mugs lie cold and fallow
Left by bursts of artistic outflow,
Whose brush reveals hints of light and shade
When on canvas, paint is gently splayed.

The Stories

are just odes or ditties,
Some might say how daft and odd it is,
The limericks are short and clever,
But others just drag on forever.

The net effect is here before you,
Take it slowly, do not just flick through,
'Tails and Verse' of great variety,
Written for children under ninety.

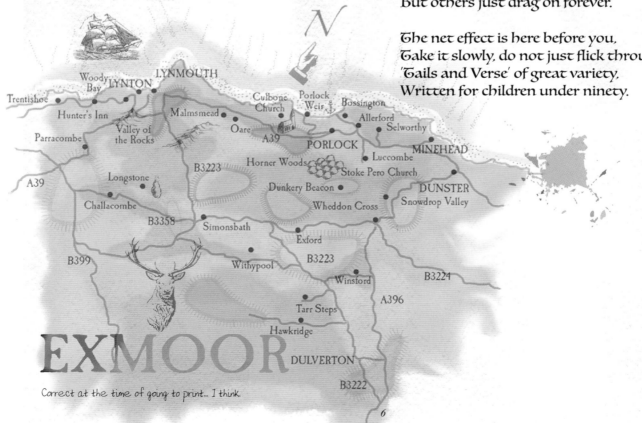

Correct at the time of going to print... I think.

Note:- *Anthropomorphic

From Greek words meaning human and shape,
A word for 'personification':
Attribute of 'things' which can escape
From beast to human, through translation.

Robertson Partridge

THE EXMOOR MAN

Bernard is a lonely man
He leads a simple life,
And he struggles, best he can
This farmer wants a wife.

Wants or needs? He is not sure;
He is stuck in his ways,
But having someone help him
Might shorten his long days.

Just a little cooking, and
Some cleaning, not too much,
Maybe warm his bed at night
And tidy up a touch.

Perhaps a bit of washing,
Ironing... well, not really,
Dinner on when he gets home?
Something he'd like dearly.

Reynard, on the other hand
Is quite the 'ladies' man';
Would fete and love the woman,
Well, that is his 'game plan'.

With the money to indulge
He'll party with the best,
Encouraging their shopping...
Yes, all their needs addressed.

He'd take them out to dinner,
Festoon them all with flowers,
Let them lay out in the sun,
Or in the bath spend hours.

He would open doors for them,
Lay his coat in puddles,
Buy satin sheets for their bed,
All this just for cuddles.

Reality is different
As happy couples know,
Farmers should be well aware,
You reap that which you sow.

Game Birds

We're three game birds of a feather
And, as such, we stick together,
And at that certain time of year
We have a heightened sense of fear.

The 'Glorious Twelfth', an odd term
The title that make game birds squirm,
An open season on the grouse
And soon on friends, an 'open house'.

Instead of long days having fun
We then spend time dodging the gun,
We don't know of rhyme nor reason
Why men have a shooting season.

A tasty morsel we may be,
But it is time we three agree
To make a stand, enough no more
We're going to even up the score.

No more ducking pellets and shot
'Enough's enough' they've had their lot,
No longer on their 'bill of fare'
They really haven't got a prayer.

For these few months our life's one aim
Is not to play their little game,
So, for us, our simple wish is
To avoid their fancy dishes.

They'll not have us bound and trussed
And roasted with a crispy crust,
On platter laid in some wine sauce,
With veg and game chips for main course.

POCKET THE BUCKSHOT

THIS BIRD'S NOT FOR STUFFING !

JUST SAY NO... to Game Pie

MAKE ♥ NOT POT ROAST

Clay Pigeons Not Game Birds

No more plucking and stuffing too
This will be our ultimate coup,
They'll not need pans, nor pots, nor grill,
Nor all their guns; we've had our fill.

Though there's no need to go without
They could just cook an extra sprout,
Or, available profusely
They could try a bowl of muesli.

Yes, we don't care what they feel like
We will from now on be on strike,
So it's heads down lads, keep your nerve
Don't give yourself as an 'hors d'oeuvre'.

We'll see you February on the first,
Positions then will be reversed,
A time we can ourselves arouse,
That is the date the law allows...

The hunting season now complete
We are no longer in retreat,
Bang! Alas they are still firing
Blast them now for not retiring.

O.K. we'll implement plan 'B'
And set aside our 'jeux d'esprit',
Their actions are unsavoury
So let's break out our armoury.

As soon as our guns are manned
We will assume the upper hand,
OK lads, let's start firing
BANG! Ha Ha; now they're retiring!

The moral of this tale is clear, It's hunters that should live in fear,
Whilst it may be a bit absurd, just do not mess with these 'Game Birds'.

'ONE IN FOUR'

"Would you drive a little slower?"
Said the tortoise to the hare,
"Those nasty bends on Porlock Hill
Give me really quite a scare.

And we should be on the Toll Road
It's a nicer, safer route."
So the tortoise cried with worry,
As the hare
depressed his foot.

"The views are well worth looking at
I assure you, guaranteed,
But we will not see anything
If we travel at this speed."

"No, Porlock Hill's the way to go
Can't believe you don't agree,
Faster, faster", yelled the hare,
"Keep your shell on, wait and see."

Tortoise, now, was shaking badly
Staring at the next bend right,
'One in four' and very scary
This would be his biggest fright.

'Low gear now and keep your distance'
Words that simply spring to mind,
But 'change up, foot down, go for it'
It's just madness unconfined.

But then the village looms in sight,
When the brakes must be applied,
They sense that smell that fills the air
Burning oil and brake pads fried.

"I think I've had enough of this,
I'm not suited to such speed,
A tortoise is slow by nature
It was long ago decreed."

And so, they reach the final straight
And come to rest quite gently,
Hare exclaimed, "Wow that was fun!"
As Tortoise left the Bentley.

OLD SCRUMPY MACK

Oh dear! What can the matter be?
Who has been at the apple tree,
Well, guess, and who else would it be?
Yes, welcome to old Scrumpy Mack.

He makes brew that's like 'Golden Fire',
With fruit purloined, or just acquired,
Fair means or foul, as it transpires,
And that's why he's called Scrumpy Mack.

Bramley, Cox and Orange Pippin,
They're all game, and ripe for nickin',
What he can, he will be strippin'
For cider, that's old Scrumpy Mack.

Mack is, some think, of ill repute,
Something he hates and will refute,
He's just acting to turn this fruit
Into cider; that's Scrumpy Mack.

Some fruit is bruised and quite battered;
Such state is really of no matter,
Big or small or a bit splattered;
It's all the same for Scrumpy Mack.

Strength not taste, is what he'll savour,
Just ignore the odd invader;
Bugs and spiders might add flavour,
Anything goes for Scrumpy Mack.

Presses, filters, checks the content,
Ignores most of the sediment,
He then waits for it to ferment,
With his feet up, that's Scrumpy Mack.

It's then put through 'Mack's inspection',
A short sip, plus some reflection,
Then bottled with some perfection,
That's job done for old Scrumpy Mack.

The strength, of course does so vary,
One bottle can be so scary,
A second, you'll be quite merry,
...Fall over like old Scrumpy Mack.

Nosey Rosie

Rosie is a dormouse,
A very sleepy thing,
She sleeps from late Autumn,
And through to early spring.

When the Spring shows its face,
Sun higher in the sky,
Rosie stirs, in her nest,
And opens up one eye.

First a yawn, then a stretch,
Not wanting to delay,
She draws her curtains back,
And looks out on the day.

Winter's gone, Spring is here,
The flowers are sun-kissed,
Staring out, and wondering
What she may have missed.

But all those things can wait
She'll do it in a while,
With other things to do,
She puts them in a pile.

Her first job is to clean,
She likes a tidy house,
Any dirt or clutter
Offends this Exmoor mouse.

So with whiskers twitching,
She sets about her chores,
Attacking them at pace,
So she can get outdoors.

She grabs her trusty broom
And sets about the floor,
Sweeping up the dust
As if she is at war.

Plus a duster in her hand,
She loves to 'multi-task',
Unlike the male dormouse,
You wouldn't even ask.

Next she cleans the windows
With verve and enterprise,
Then into the kitchen,
Which gives up no surprise.

She gathers up her post
That's piled up by the door,
Many bills and flyers
Are covering the floor.

Spring then turns to Summer,
The friends are feeling free,
Reality though dawns
Whilst on their woodland spree.

Their seasons are so short,
She has to concentrate,
Food is quite important,
She must accumulate.

So then it's back to work
To gather in supplies,
Food she needs for Winter
Upon which she relies.

With the Autumn waning
When days are past their best,
She makes final plans for
Another six months rest.

All things neat and tidy
With everything just right,
Windows shut and doors locked,
Then Rosie says...

"Goodnight... zzzzzz"

There's mould upon the bread,
The milk is past its best,
Green bits on the jam and
The butter has 'gone west'.

All unacceptable -
Not Rosie's 'cup of tea',
She has a strict maxim,
Appearances are key.

Back into her bedroom,
She makes a new straw bed,
She changes all the sheets
And tries to get ahead.

Only when she's finished
And things are nearly done,
Can she then consider
Going out for some sun.

It's then she can relax,
Go off and see some friends,
Time to play and frolic
Until the season ends.

ORDER OF THE COURTS

*W*e know 'Bo Peep',
Who lost her sheep
And didn't know where to turn, so,
*C*alled Turk & Hare,
They know what's where,
But only for a 'return', though.

*Y*es Turk & Hare,
Being aware,
Will find what you need anyway,
*T*hey have a good feel
For a great deal,
Providing you're willing to pay.

*T*wo legs or four
They know the score,
They'll acquire them dead or alive,
*W*hole, boned or skinned,
Flat, rolled or pinned,
As you want them, they will arrive.

WAN
A
Turk
'THE SC

Any information received will

TED

s ——

Hare

NDRELS'

They know what's what,
And how to spot
The best deal the market can do,
Slide them a note,
And they will quote,
To match them, there are very few.

They've got a line
On some 'bent' wine,
Plus whisky, gin, vodka or rum,
You want a case?
They know the place,
They'll get it all for the right sum.

They keep their stash
And back up cash,
In a hole close to Robber's Bridge,
Where they've set snares
To guard their wares,
And passers-by they'll discourage.

They buy and sell
And do quite well,
Not always quite within the law,
'Wide Boys' they be,
And they'll stay free
Till men in blue knock on their door.

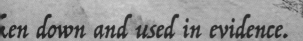

en down and used in evidence.

Ode to Rodney

If you go down to the woods today
Be sure of a big surprise,
For it's not bears that come out to play,
It's Rodney for his supplies.

He will be there, right in his best spot
Watching for pricks and scratches,
All the best blackberries he will pick
For jam, he'll boil up in batches.

He gropes and picks, ignoring the pain
And samples some of his forage,
For him it's worth the struggle for gain
And the jam that goes on his porridge.

The best of fruit, nothing to grumble
He's driven by dreams of pies,
And then a thought... 'blackberry crumble'
Appears in front of his eyes.

So off he goes, contented and proud,
His pick of the day on board,
His back weighed down, his head held unbowed,
...Rodney has got his reward.

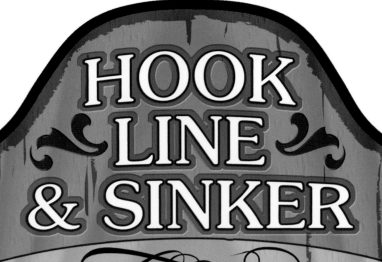

HOOK LINE & SINKER

They do say that catching crabs is
Like sitting and watching paint dry,
Just staring into space for hours
For that welcome bite, by and by.

But Barry was a patient chap
And loved just being outdoors,
He had everything he needed,
Just purchased from 'The Harbour Stores'.

And Suddenly…
It took it hook line and sinker
And was lifted out on the quay,
Then gently placed in the bucket,
Barry had the first for his tea….

So, British Crabbing Week started,
An annual event at The Weir,
They would turn out in their numbers,
In all weathers they'd persevere.

They'd also know the problems there,
As they are clearly notified,
The sea gulls are inquisitive and
There's a dodgy, quick rising tide.

The choice of bait they knew was 'key'
And a big consideration,
What is the best way to attract
An inquisitive crustacean?

Barry preferred good old lugworm,
But some thought a different way,
Chicken neck, raw fish or bacon,
Were all on the menu today.

At close, Barry counted his catch,
Which he thought, for the day, was fair,
Now he was faced with decision,
Let them go, or 'Crab Meunière'?

He had to toil with his conscience
And the culinary delights,
He decided that, in all fairness,
Even crabs had family and rights.

He watched as these little fellows
Crawled over the stones to the sea,
Then home, quite content with himself,
…Peanut butter on toast for tea.

From the crab's point of view

As a harmless crustacean, I just loathe the sensation
when caught on the blighter's line,
And the utter deflation, when, in time resignation
the day is on the decline,
Then there's sudden elation and some mass celebration,
as we're thrown back into the brine.

One for the Pot

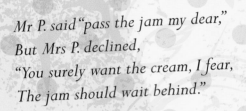

In life there are many choices,
And discussions ensue,
Which may result in raised voices,
When folk get in a stew.

THE STORY...

The 'P.'s went out for tea one day
And found a nice quaint spot,
Fine starched linen and cake display,
'Twas called 'One for the Pot'.

The list of teas was appealing,
The range of cakes quite vast,
They served Assam and Darjeeling,
Some Herbal and Breakfast.

Mrs P. chose cream tea with jam
And a pot of Oolong,
Mr P. the same with Assam:
Black blend, it's not so strong.

Mrs P. scorned his selection,
"Not a good choice of blend."
Mr P. said, on reflection,
"Madam - don't condescend."

They placed their order and waited,
Tea and scones then appeared,
"Service a little belated!"
A fact Mrs P. volunteered.

Mr P. said "pass the jam my dear,"
But Mrs P. declined,
"You surely want the cream, I fear,
The jam should wait behind."

"Have you gone raving mad," he cursed,
Poor Mr P., distraught,
"I've always put the jam on first,
That's just how I was taught."

"Well you are wrong, you should have known,"
Mrs P. directed,
"To start, the cream goes on the scone,
Protocol corrected."

"My goodness, woman, you bang on,
Don't lecture me on taste,
The thing you hold is called a scone,
Apologise with haste."

THE MORAL...

Just go out to tea for a laugh,
Stick with the local brew,
Take your 'bun' and break it in half,
Spread what you want - we do!

The B&B

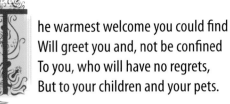

The warmest welcome you could find
Will greet you and, not be confined
To you, who will have no regrets,
But to your children and your pets.

Though children should be seen not heard
And dogs on beds are not preferred,
And careful where you hang wet macs,
Except for those, the rules are lax.

Feather pillows and cotton sheets,
Springy mattress, bathroom en-suite,
Her B&B, quite distinguished,
And she does serve great 'Full English'.

An early call she can provide,
Just let her know when you decide,
And if you're home in time for tea
Join her for a small sweet sherry.

There is no fuss at breakfast time,
Just Mrs B's eggs; quite sublime
And your taste buds to awaken;
Try her local home cured bacon.

But continental she won't serve;
No smelly cheese and them 'hors d'oeuvres',
Croissants and stuff – not for this host,
You'll have to stick to British toast.

Bring your wellies, your boots and bikes,
Your walking poles or climbing spikes,
Then step out onto moorland wild,
By views prepare to be beguiled.

An evening meal on your return
And hot cocoa as you adjourn,
She wants you to enjoy your stay
And then come back another day.

So there you have the full PR,
About the best there is, by far,
Set in Porlock, 'where moor meets sea',
A celebrated hostelry.

L·O·S·T
ON EXMOOR

Out and about with

William J. Bird
&
Randolph Pecker

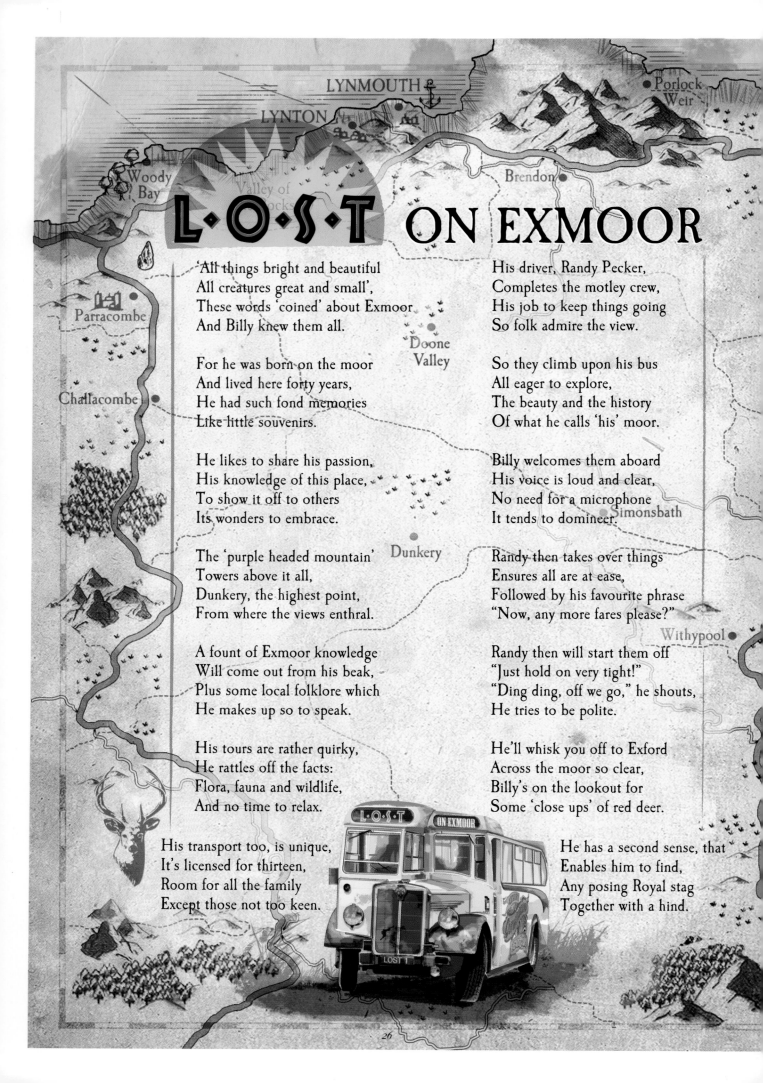

L·O·S·T ON EXMOOR

'All things bright and beautiful
All creatures great and small',
These words 'coined' about Exmoor
And Billy knew them all.

For he was born on the moor
And lived here forty years,
He had such fond memories
Like little souvenirs.

He likes to share his passion,
His knowledge of this place,
To show it off to others
Its wonders to embrace.

The 'purple headed mountain'
Towers above it all,
Dunkery, the highest point,
From where the views enthral.

A fount of Exmoor knowledge
Will come out from his beak,
Plus some local folklore which
He makes up so to speak.

His tours are rather quirky,
He rattles off the facts:
Flora, fauna and wildlife,
And no time to relax.

His transport too, is unique,
It's licensed for thirteen,
Room for all the family
Except those not too keen.

His driver, Randy Pecker,
Completes the motley crew,
His job to keep things going
So folk admire the view.

So they climb upon his bus
All eager to explore,
The beauty and the history
Of what he calls 'his' moor.

Billy welcomes them aboard
His voice is loud and clear,
No need for a microphone
It tends to domineer.

Randy then takes over things
Ensures all are at ease,
Followed by his favourite phrase
"Now, any more fares please?"

Randy then will start them off
"Just hold on very tight!"
"Ding ding, off we go," he shouts,
He tries to be polite.

He'll whisk you off to Exford
Across the moor so clear,
Billy's on the lookout for
Some 'close ups' of red deer.

He has a second sense, that
Enables him to find,
Any posing Royal stag
Together with a hind.

LUXURY OUTWARDBOUND SAFARI TOURS

BILLY BIRD

RANDY PECKER

Randy's quite responsive too
When great sights come around,
One look from dear old Billy,
A stopping place is found.

Quickly Randy stops the bus
Then Billy points out where,
The cameras then can capture
The wonder of the pair.

Next, on to Exford Common
A favourite grazing place,
To see some Exmoor Ponies
Close up, and 'face to face'.

Before the weather changes
They head toward the coast,
To take in stunning views
That leave them quite engrossed.

At the Valley of the Rocks
A herd of feral goats,
And ice age rock formations
About which poets wrote.

Returning through Doone Valley,
Oare Church and Robber's Bridge,
And to take some 'snaps' of a
Lasting Exmoor image.

Turning back to base again
As daylight starts to fade,
Billy gives his closing speech
About what's been surveyed.

So happy little trippers,
Tired, but well rewarded,
Sit back for the final leg
Exmoor now recorded.

CONTINUED...

27

DEFINITELY NOT DRAWN TO SCALE

HOWEVER...

William's transport's not so hot
And trips could be cut short,
There is a minor issue
Of quite a major sort.

His 'Luxury' Outward bound
Safari Transport coach,
Has a habit to break down
It's not beyond reproach.

Now, an open top tourer
Sounds perfect for the role,
Sun and light, breeze through your hair
Delightful on the whole.

But breaking down on Exmoor
When day comes to a close,
One should try avoiding, it's
Not something I'd propose.

That's where Randy's skill is used,
A feather in his cap,
There is nothing he can't fix
Whilst Billy gives them chat.

So Billy's, always cheerful,
Hands round some mugs of tea,
And those furry mittens that
He always finds handy.

He keeps the punters happy,
Yes, that is Billy's plan,
'Cos rain and force nine winds don't
Defeat the 'Exmoor Man'.

Darkness falls, the bus is fixed,
Randy has delivered,
On Exmoor you're looked after
...Don't be 'lily livered'.

ENTITLES ONE L·O·S·T ON EXMOOR
· COMPLIMENTARY HOT COCOA ·

POST SCRIPT:
Those who booked through Mrs B.
Will still get their cocoa,
For no-one is let down here
There's always 'quid pro quo'.

THE END

LUXURY OUTWARDBOUND SAFARI TOURS

L·O·S·T

NOTES ON BEHALF OF

The Red Deer...

"What I always find amazing
When I am just simply grazing,
Is all the many folk that stare,
And take photos they then can share
With all their many mates back home,
I think it's called 'tourist syndrome'.

But I'm content to simply stand
For my fine features to be scanned,
I might indeed strike a proud pose
A haughty look with turned up nose,
But if I'm quite honest with you
My dear friend Billy pays me to.

The Exmoor ponies 'cross the moor
Have sought a similar rapport,
Not sure about their 'bottom line'
I trust it's not as much as mine,
Let's face it... what's the better 'catch'?
A giant stag or horse with thatch.

The feral goats are quite a draw
Though I'm not sure they know the score,
I am convinced they make no gains
They haven't got the business brains,
They may hold out a begging box
Because life's tough out on those rocks."

The Exmoor Pony...

"Our dear friend Stag thinks he's so cool
But we just subtly play the fool,
Our 'deal' with Billy does us proud
Because he knows we draw a crowd,
Yes we can bargain, make a fuss,
There are you see, a lot of us.

On all us ponies Bill relies
We're always there with soulful eyes,
When Stag's away we spread around
To cover most of moorland ground,
We're always there, there's no mystique,
And on Exmoor we are unique."

The Feral Goats...

"Why such a great big deal on this?
Old Bill would never be remiss,
Not to pay up for protection
When he is in our direction,
For what would all his trippers think
Say, if his bus went on the 'blink'
Quite so far away from base,
A breakdown...
...Oh! what a disgrace."

They call me Mr Pleasant.
Hello, how do you do?
I am a wandering pheasant,
And what they say is true.

I give help around the moor
To those who are in need,
And I try to reassure,
But nothing's guaranteed.

It's just a great existence
With which I am content,
And with simple sustenance,
From me, there's no dissent.

Just give me little creatures
That really need my aid,
And all the moorland features,
'Round which, my life I've made.

For some this life is boring,
They complicate it so,
For me, it is restoring,
So, where else would I go?

My Life is here on Exmoor,
I'll stay here by and by,
And sleep, you can be sure,
Beneath its dark night sky.

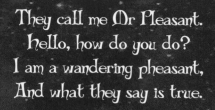

They call me
Mr Pleasant

Sultry Poultry

The chickens languished in the yard,
It was too hot for poultry,
The weatherman had got it wrong,
It was quite close and sultry.

They had finished with their laying,
In this heat it wasn't fair,
It's bad enough when eggs are round,
But, today they felt like square.

The Oyster SHACK
Porlock Bay

I am a Bivalve Mollusc; that's
An Oyster by the way!
I'm living, in a bed, with friends,
Just here in Porlock Bay.

We're part of an experiment,
But we don't mind one bit,
It's nice to lie in bed all day,
We freely do admit.

The local Porlock Company
Looks after us so well,
As 'grade A' Pacific Oysters,
Our qualities excel.

They say we are 'sustainable';
I don't know what they mean,
But we filter lots of water
From which, our food, we glean.

Our statistics are amazing,
So much we can filter,
A dozen gallons by the hour!
Shows that we're in kilter.

We used to have some neighbours when
Some mussels lived next door,
But we've been told, some seagulls came...
We don't see them no more.

My mates and I, though, are O.K.
All chilling by the beach,
Just far enough away from harm,
And safely out of reach.

So we're alright and comfortable,
But need to grow some more,
We're ready when we're four years old,
But I'm not sure what for.

Though rumour has it, when we're big,
We have to leave the Bay,
But we are quite excited; it
Must mean a holiday.

We will get to visit Porlock
And places far away,
Go to pubs, hotels and restaurants,
And 'chill out' every day.

AH WELL,
THAT'S THE DREAM!
FOR NOW, IT'S A GREAT LIFE
BEING A 'GRADE A'
PACIFIC OYSTER!

33

The Fox's Tale
"Tally Ho!"

'A hunting we will go,
a hunting we will go,
Heigh ho, the dairy-o,
a hunting we will go!
We'll catch a fox
and put him in a box,
And then we'll let him go!'

...Or so they thought;

For Archie was a sly old fox
And of quite a different sort,
He had been hunted now for years,
And never close to being caught.

He knew the moors, the woods and streams
And enjoyed his weekly outing,
At all times he was elusive,
Of that there could be no doubting.

Old Archie has written three books
About his many successes,
A fox has to make a living
And income, from sales, progresses.

He'd wake early on hunting day
A good breakfast, and time to plan,
Bits of his scheme would be in place
With Jeffrey, his trusted 'point man'.

Green jacket, his jodpurs and boots
He'd always dress for the part,
And would be completely prepared
In time for the ten-thirty start.

He knew where they would hold their 'meet'
It was published in the 'Free Press',
He would then hang around, just in sight,
So their numbers he could assess.

He loved to see them all dressed up
Preparing themselves for the chase,
How prim and proper they all looked
Astride their steeds with such grace.

This week Archie spied a large crowd
He knew it would be a good 'hunt',
But, with his great planning, he knew
He'd always be way out in front.

He made his way up on Ley Hill
From where he could see their first moves,
He heard the horn cry out in joy,
Baying pack and sound of the hooves.

So he set off down to the woods
To the stream and his crossing place,
Sitting for a short time, waiting,
Ensuring a scent they could trace.

He then crossed the water quickly
Confusing the scent for a time,
So the hounds did not know at first
If they were to swim or to climb.

He sprinted then to Webbers Post
A tight little path for the pack,
Then over the hill to Cloutsham
His intention to double back.

Over the 'Ball' and down the hill
Criss-crossing the stream all the way,
Fluid and graceful his movements
As if he were in a ballet.

34

Before he got to the bottom
He paused, and listened, then stood still,
Heard the faint sound of pursuers
Then broke left, and ran up the hill.

Over the hill and cross the road
Where he stopped at a local farm,
Then, at the front door he waited
For a while, all was quite calm.

Now he could hear the hounds nearing
And the horses not far away,
He hoped his timing was perfect
For the 'trump card' he would now play.

He then heard Jeffrey arriving
So ready to make his last move,
His plan now was almost complete,
He had nothing further to prove.

The farmhouse door then flew open
And Archie was in down the hall,
Then right through, out of the back door
And closed it, the chase to forestall.

The hounds all rushed in the hallway
But found the back door was now closed,
Chaos then reigned in the household
So Archie just left unopposed.

His friend had arrived right on cue
In a cloud of diesel and fumes,
A tractor-trailer full of hay
Wherein, his spot Archie assumes.

Then Jeffrey drove off down the lane,
Horses and hounds couldn't follow,
So a quiet drive from now on
With Archie back to his hollow.

Now hidden from view, the trail cut,
Their hunt had come to a halt,
A great result for our hero...
This pack was just not worth their salt.

So that's another hunt finished
And nobody hurt, so that's fine,
Into his chair with his note book
And a lovely glass of red wine.

35

The Exmoor Pedestrian

A Tribute to

Walkers, Ramblers, Hikers, Trekkers, Climbers, Strollers, Back Packers, Runners, Joggers, Yompers, Footsloggers, Rovers, Drifters, Wayfarers...

They do the grand tour
By foot, that is sure,
Diverse types galore,
Below, as disclosed...

Some '**back pack**' the moor,
They like to explore,
The pain they ignore;
They must walk the most.

Kagouls they adore
And thick socks what's more,
So warmth they may store,
If they're so disposed.

Some '**jog**' till they're sore,
The looks that they draw,
Though some just ignore,
As if they're opposed.

And '**trekkers**' galore
Abound on the moor,
So brace yourself for
This gathering host.

They '**hike**' on the moor,
A circular tour,
For they can endure
And then make the boast.

With map or brochure
Might help to ensure,
They cover the moor
From 'pillar to post'.

The '**runners**' keep score
As they hit the moor,
A long ragged corps:
Aim? 'First past the post'.

The hills on the moor,
Provide the allure,
That '**climbers**' go for
And head for the coast.

They don their boots, or
Their feet might get sore,
And walking poles cure
That stumble - almost.

'**Dog walks**' on the moor,
To some, it's a chore,
But most do adore
And get quite engrossed.

Some '**ramble**' the moor,
Dressed in 'Haute Couture'.
They think they're top-drawer
And suitably posed.

Some '**wander**' the moor,
There are hills that lure,
But if they're unsure,
They don't get exposed.

Folk '**stroll**' on the moor,
It's all they want for;
On Sunday, what's more,
Then home for their roast.

But one things for sure,
And I underscore,
Please, just look out for
The list on this post.

BEWARE
Notice to Pedestrians
Tics, snakes, ponies, deer, AND some locals may bite.

The games we play...

On Monday they play Skittles,
On Tuesday it is Darts,
Then Wednesday they have Cribbage,
Though, just in fits and starts.

On Thursday, out come Lie Dice,
Which can last all night through,
That takes them to Friday, which
They generally eschew.

Friday is… well… Fish & Chips
Without the normal game,
'Cos once a month there's Quiz Night
So that's what gets the blame.

Saturday, they play Poker,
Though not their cup of tea,
Sometimes it's Bar Billiards
But only when it's free.

Then, at last, it's Sunday night
Four players in the frame,
It draws the biggest crowd, for
This is a high stakes game.

Sunday's match is serious,
It's highlight of the week,
Tension is quite palpable,
They hardly dare to speak.

The crowd all gather near for
The next of their conflicts,
This gladitorial stage,
Set for the double six.

The umpire reads out the rules,
Which everybody knows!
Then the gloves are off at last,
…The guys play *Dominoes*.

GERALD'S TAIL
TRADITIONAL ENGLISH ALE

The Ship Inn

A 'Pot Man' a 'Cellar Man'
Works hard to fill the jaws
Of the thirsty folk upstairs,
A martyr to his cause.

Rarely seen, or considered
By all the drinking hoards,
As he performs his duties
Down there beneath the boards.

It's not without its upside,
For Gerald likes a drink,
Tasting is part of the job,
Or so he'd like to think.

He's happy humping barrels,
It just builds up a thirst
And when they're in position,
He has to try them first.

'Tween his toils with pipes and bungs
And ever changing kegs,
He'll empty all used glasses
And finish off the dregs.

Old Gerald calls this 'spillage',
His job, of course, to clean,
To him it doesn't matter
Too much where it has been.

He knows someone must do it
Though it's a bit mundane,
The perks are not too bad, so...
He'll do it all again.

CARPENTERS
PLUMBERS
& ELECTRICIANS

Squeaky, Leaky, and Mr Sparks

CERTIFIED
CONTRACTORS TO THE
CONSTRUCTION INDUSTRY.

INVOICE
OFFICE No.

M _____   DATE _____   YEAR _____

FREE ESTIMATES

We all need quality workmen,
That's unless we're a handy man,
But finding the right sort of chap
Is the heart of any game plan.

In our village though, there is one,
Well, it's not one really, but three,
It's just that they turn up 'en bloc',
Which day? There is no guarantee.

They will all arrive in their van,
The pride of their motoring fleet,
Exuding style and confidence
And a look that is very discreet.

Their skills are well tried and tested,
Their work is a real *'tour de force'*,
But for those who're not satisfied,
Note their terms state...
                    "...without recourse".

Squeaky, Leaky and Mr Sparks
The finest of artisan men,
They'll be there to start work at 9
But stop for their tea about 10.

A smoke outside at 11
And their lunch from 12 until 2,
More tea is requested at 4,
Then at 5, they say "that'll do."

Squeaky's a wood working scholar,
A marvel with hammer and nails,
He never uses a set square
And struggles with all that entails.

Leaky is a plumber... sort of,
Well at least he works with pipes,
He was a car exhaust fitter,
And that is how he earned his stripes.

Now Mr Sparks is, well guess what...
Yes! An electrician...of sorts,
Whose type of wire installation
Is the furthest thing from your thoughts.

No job is too big or too small,
They'll give you a quote on the spot,
But don't expect a quick finish...
And a start is quite a long shot.

They're slow and they argue a bit
And stop when they hear the kettle,
The only thing they do quickly...
Invoice, and ask you to settle.

Our expertise is our guarantee, we don't do 'Plan B'.

Cycle~Ology

There are different cyclists that traverse the moor,
The mode does depend on what they want it for.

They are readily split, for ease, into three,
And I will describe them with alacrity.

There's the...
Lycra Bikers,
Social Cyclers,
Mucky Mountaineers.

Who are, by type...
Fast and furious,
Quaint and curious,
Riders without fears.

Neat gear shifters,
Near lane drifters,
Pathway commandeers.

With...
Go faster stripes,
Lights of all types,
Mud behind the ears.

Whose style is ...
Frightening speed,
Simply proceed,
Breaking more frontiers.

Riding high stakes,
Careful with brakes,
It will end in tears.

Slim alloy wheels,
Comfort appeals,
Such wild buccaneers.

Slick, speedy tyres,
All it requires,
Keeping up with peers.

Carbon fibre,
Ride provider,
Rough ground pioneers.

Pedal with zeal,
Gently free wheel,
All blood, sweat and tears.

Their attitude to safety...
Centre pull brakes,
As long as it takes,
Downhill it careers.

Ride the fast lane,
Gentle restrain,
Cycling cavaliers.

Past in a flash,
Try not to crash,
Dents are souvenirs.

Banana hats,
Nice riding caps,
Something that adheres.

Reading last rights,
Sensible lights,
Out searching frontiers.

For maintenance...
Wheel, quick release,
Just elbow grease,
Any volunteers?

How slick is that?
Well, that fell flat.
Let's have a few beers.

And they carry...
Drink carrier,
Luggage pannier,
No, it interferes.

Summary...
They'll never quit,
Oh well that's it,
And it just appears...

From nowhere !!!

Duck Race
On the Sparkhayes Stream

There was a young duckling called Pete,
Who had most amazing webbed feet,
But this duck, the poor schmuck,
Wasn't 'Aylesbury', bad luck,
So his pedigree wasn't complete.

But then at the annual duck race,
What joy it would bring to his face,
He would burst down the stream
With a full head of steam,
And would always come in first place.

So breeding's not all that's required,
The 'private school' duck had retired,
'Twas hard graft and training
Without the complaining,
And a yen for success that's 'hot-wired'.

Salty &
the 'Waterfront Gang'

> "...'TWAS A MOST TERRIBLE NIGHT
> AND THE WIND WAS BLOWING FORCE 8,
> THE SEAS WERE HEAVY AND FIERCE,
> IT WAS HARD TO STEER THE BOAT STRAIGHT.
>
> THE RAIN WAS LASHING MY FACE
> AND MY EYES WERE SMARTING WITH PAIN,
> HUGE WAVES BROKE OVER THE BOW
> AND MY ARMS WERE FEELING THE STRAIN..."

...AND SO THE STORY GOES ON

As the skipper recounted his tales,
Of daring exploits at sea,
Of the cold, the rain and the gales.

Folk all listened intently
To the deeds of him and his crew,
They so enjoyed the telling,
Though most doubted any were true.

Salty was there every day,
In The Ship, a pint in his hand,
The way he spoke, you'd guess that
He spent little time on dry land.

But his boat 'Ocean Express',
A name that sums up 'a sure thing',
On which he lived all the time,
Was never seen off its mooring.

Then when he'd finished his tale,
He'd exclaim "I must catch the tide",
But then return in a while
'Landlocked' as the harbour had dried.

"Hail and rain! I've missed the tide,
Must change the ship's watch, deary dear.
Never mind! Now where was I?
Oh yes... and can I have a beer?"

And so he would continue
Until closing time and some more,
But even in The Ship Inn
He'd be pointed soon to the door.

Then he'd stagger to his boat
Quite apparently 'Mal de Mer',
Gently board his vessel and
Then sink into his 'Captain's Chair'.

In morning watch, at 'Six Bells'
He'd be up and very alert,
He'd dreamt about some crisis
Which he'd managed, just, to avert.

Next day he told them about
His time in the 'Roaring Forties',
And when he went round Cape Horn,
A gem of his sailing sorties.

They all enjoyed every phrase;
'Cut and run', then 'anchors aweigh',
'Batten down the hatches' and
'Let's make sail' and 'get underway'!

44

Meanings are not always clear
Although they would never confide,
They would listen intently
Even after he'd missed the tide.

What is 'the cut of your jib'?
'Fathom out', 'on your starboard side',
'Ship shape and Bristol fashion',
All this and it's still at low tide.

Then he would 'push the boat out',
More beer he would bring 'alongside',
When they're 'three sheets to the wind',
No one cares if they've missed the tide.

When done, he'd be off once more,
All beaming and smiling with pride,
They knew he'd be back again,
'Hard and fast', when he'd missed the tide.

His friends, 'The Water Front Gang',
Would wait for him, all bleary eyed,
Puffing pipes in The Ship Inn,
'Cos they knew he would miss the tide!

The days and tales continue, with Salty, pint pot at his side,
To all those who would listen... *but he always would miss the tide!*

"*Nurses are angels in comfortable shoes*"

AUTHOR UNKNOWN

NURSE BABS

Her bicycle is very old
But not as old as she,
She acquired it from a vicar,
When he came round for tea.

It's served its purpose very well,
It's solid and quite firm,
Already lasted many years
And might be round long term.

You know the type 'sit up and beg',
Like Grandma used to ride,
A cover for her back wheel, so
Her skirt's not caught inside.

Great big mud guards and chain cover,
With '3 speed' gears as well,
Squeaky side-pull lever brakes and,
Importantly, a bell.

Her basket sits on, proud up front,
Filled with her tools of trade,
And with a thermos flask of tea,
In case she gets delayed.

For our dear Babs, the district nurse,
Does need to get around,
And she finds this mode of transport
Particularly sound.

It's very necessary when
She travels to her calls,
Tending to the sick and needy,
Wherever illness falls.

But roads on Exmoor are quite steep,
Sometimes she can't make it,
So then, she will get off and push
It's either that or quit.

But it's different going downhill,
Its great the way she feels,
She lifts her feet up in the air
And, down the hill, free wheels.

'Twenty-Four-Seven' she's on-call
For fevers and for sprains,
And for young expectant mothers,
Who suffer labour pains.

Those who are quite elderly, get
A visit from dear Babs;
When she comes to administer
The normal winter jabs.

She's also needed to perform
Some things quite 'intrusive',
Her tasks we know are varied, and
Can seem quite abusive.

She'd extract something from her bag,
"A sample", she'd implore,
"Now don't flush or feel embarrassed,
I've seen it all before."

With children she's a real soft touch,
She bribes them with nice treats,
Giving nasty medicine with
Some chocolate or boiled sweets.

Pineapple chunks, sherbet lemons,
Plus all sorts in her jar,
They take away the nasty taste…
Best medicine by far.

And when the day is over, with
Her cup of malted milk,
She finishes her notes off and
Then curls up with her quilt.

Scary Mary

Scary Mary quite contrary
My how your powers grow,
With herbal brews,
And tea leaf news
And concoctions you can bestow.

The remedies for all those ills,
The cures for colds and flus,
Your palm reading
Quite misleading,
And those Tarot cards that you use.

The hocus pocus that goes on,
The spirits that you call,
Vodka and gin
Or 'Mickey Finn',
And that 'eye' is a crystal ball.

But our Mary is not scary,
She's sweet as apple pie,
She's kind of thought
And a good sport,
It's just that bright glint in her eye.

THE EXMOOR BEAST

"They seek him here,
they seek him there,
They seek him everywhere."

Is it black or grey, or big, or small?
Are its eyes so piercing bright?
It's never spotted in the day,
Only ever seen at night.

It scours the moorland scene, we're told,
Causing havoc all about,
But the tales have not been proven
Beyond reasonable doubt.

Some farmers have lost animals
Stories like this just abound,
But of proof, there's simply nothing,
No good evidence is found.

So myth and fable, real and true,
Folklore, maybe illusion?
Is it a fact or fantasy
All wrapped up in confusion?

Yes the creature that we speak of
Is the famous Exmoor Beast,
Of which no pictures, verified,
Until now, have been released.

You see it here in menacing pose
All those years it's been concealed,
And on this very page, a first,
It's the Exmoor Beast revealed.

You can now gaze into those eyes,
See unbridled aggression.
But underneath that blackened cloak,
Lies what? Now that's the question...

Well, that's it, finished, finito,
All wrapped up and put to bed,
It's left you wanting more I hope,
I wonder?... Leave that unsaid.

But I had a verse planned about
Maurice, a cute little mole,
And all the things he got up to
Down in the depths of his hole.

But my publisher said "no way,
I know you've been on it for ages,
It is after all quite rude,
And we have now run out of pages."

So...
You'll have to wait for the next book
Of quirky stories in rhyme,
Now the editor's on my back,
Cutting me off in my pri

The End

Robertson Partridge